WILLIAMS-SONOMA

Seasonal Favorites

The Best of Autumn & Winter
in the Seasonal Collection

Recipes by JOANNE WEIR

Photographs by PENINA

Contents

Grilled Bread with Shell Beans and Escarole

1 lb fresh shell beans, such as cranberry, lima, or flageolet

3 cloves garlic, minced

2 tablespoons chopped fresh sage

3 tablespoons extra-virgin olive oil, plus olive oil for brushing

Salt and freshly ground black pepper

18 slices country-style bread, about 3 inches in diameter

½ head escarole, cored and cut into strips 1 inch wide

1 tablespoon red wine vinegar

Small pinch of red pepper flakes

Shell the beans. Bring a saucepan three-fourths full of water to a boil over medium-high heat. Add the beans and cook until very soft, about 20 minutes. Drain, reserving 1 cup of the cooking liquid.

Preheat a broiler. In a frying pan over medium heat, combine the beans, garlic, sage, and 2 tablespoons of the oil. Cook, mashing the beans with a spoon and adding the reserved cooking liquid as needed until a rough paste forms, 10–15 minutes. Remove from the heat and continue mashing the beans to form a smooth paste. Season the mixture to taste with salt and black pepper.

Lightly brush the bread slices on both sides with oil and place on the broiler pan. Broil, turning once, until golden on both sides, 30–60 seconds on each side.

In another frying pan over high heat, warm the remaining 1 tablespoon oil. Add the escarole and cook until wilted, 2–3 minutes. Add the vinegar and red pepper flakes and season to taste with salt and black pepper. Mix well.

To serve, spread the bean purée on the toasted bread, dividing it evenly. Top with the wilted escarole and serve immediately. *Serves 6*

Mushroom and Stilton Galette

1/4 oz dried wild mushrooms such as porcini, shiitakes, or chanterelles

1 cup boiling water

2 tablespoons unsalted butter

3/4 cup sliced green onions

1 clove garlic, minced

1/2 teaspoon chopped fresh rosemary

1/2 teaspoon chopped fresh thyme

1/2 lb assorted fresh wild mushrooms such as porcini, shiitakes, and chanterelles, brushed clean and large mushrooms thinly sliced

1/2 lb fresh white mushrooms, brushed clean and thinly sliced

Sour Cream Pastry, page 60

5 oz Stilton or other good-quality blue cheese

Place the dried mushrooms in a bowl and add the boiling water. Let stand for 30 minutes until softened. Drain the mushrooms and mince finely. Preheat an oven to 400°F.

In a large frying pan over medium heat, melt the butter. Add the green onions and sauté, stirring occasionally, until soft, about 5 minutes. Add the garlic, rosemary, and thyme and continue to cook, stirring, for 1 minute longer. Raise the heat to high, add the fresh and rehydrated mushrooms, and sauté until the mushrooms are tender and the liquid they released has completely evaporated, 8–10 minutes. Transfer to a plate and let cool.

Make the pastry. On a floured work surface, roll out the pastry into a 12-inch round. Transfer to an ungreased baking sheet. Crumble the blue cheese into a bowl, add to it the cooled mushrooms and stir well. Spread the mixture over the dough, leaving a 1 1/2-inch border. Fold the dough border over the mushrooms and cheese, pleating the edge to make it fit. The center will be open.

Bake until golden brown, 30–40 minutes. Remove from the oven, let stand for 5 minutes, then slide the galette onto a serving plate. Cut into wedges and serve hot, warm, or at room temperature. *Serves 6*

Oysters on the Half Shell with Mignonette Sauce

FOR THE
MIGNONETTE SAUCE

½ cup dry red wine

3–4 tablespoons red wine vinegar

4 shallots, minced

⅛ teaspoon red pepper flakes

Freshly cracked black pepper

Crushed or shaved ice

36 oysters in the shell

Lemon wedges

Flat-leaf parsley sprigs

To make the mignonette sauce, in a bowl, stir together the wine, 3 tablespoons vinegar, shallots, red pepper flakes, and black pepper. Taste and add more vinegar if needed.

Place the bowl of mignonette sauce on a platter and surround it with a bed of ice. Discard any oysters that do not close tightly to the touch. Scrub each oyster thoroughly with a stiff-bristled brush, rinsing it well under cold running water.

Holding each oyster flat side up in a kitchen towel and using an oyster knife, slip the tip of the knife into the shell near the hinge and pry upward to open. Run the knife blade along the inside of the top shell to sever the muscle that joins the shells, then lift off the top shell. Run the knife underneath the oyster to free it from the rounded, bottom shell, being careful not to spill the liquor. Nest the oysters in their bottom shells on the ice.

Garnish the platter with lemon wedges and parsley sprigs and serve immediately. *Serves 6*

Smoked Trout in Endive Spears

1/4 cup mayonnaise

6 green onions, thinly sliced

2 small cloves garlic, minced

1 1/2 teaspoons fresh lemon juice

1/8 teaspoon ground cayenne pepper

1/2 teaspoon sweet paprika

Salt and freshly ground black pepper

1 1/2 cups flaked smoked trout fillet

4 heads Belgian endive

Lemon wedges

In a small bowl, combine the mayonnaise, green onions, garlic, lemon juice, cayenne, paprika, and salt and black pepper to taste. Mix well. Add the trout and stir to combine.

Cut off the base from each endive and separate the heads into individual spears. Use only the larger endive spears; reserve the smaller ones for another use.

Using the broad end of each endive spear, scoop up a heaping teaspoonful of the trout mixture, then spread it along the spears with a knife. Arrange on a platter and garnish with lemon wedges. Serve immediately. *Serves 6*

Parsnip and Carrot Soup

1½ tablespoons
unsalted butter

1 yellow onion,
chopped

1¼ lb small parsnips,
peeled and coarsely
chopped

1 lb carrots, peeled
and coarsely chopped

6 cups chicken stock

4 cups water

Salt and freshly
ground pepper

FOR THE YOGURT
GARNISH

⅓ cup plain yogurt

About 2 tablespoons
milk

Salt and freshly
ground pepper

1½ tablespoons
chopped fresh
flat-leaf parsley

In a large soup pot over medium heat, melt the butter. Add
the onion and sauté, stirring occasionally, until soft, about
10 minutes. Raise the heat to high, add the parsnips, carrots,
stock, and water and bring to a boil. Reduce the heat to
medium-low and simmer, uncovered, until the vegetables
are tender, about 30 minutes.

Using a blender and working in batches, purée the soup
on high speed until smooth, 3–4 minutes for each batch. Strain
through a fine-mesh sieve into a clean soup pot. Place over low
heat and reheat to serving temperature. Season to taste with
salt and pepper.

While the soup is heating, make the yogurt garnish: In a
small bowl, whisk together the yogurt and enough milk to
make a barely fluid paste. Season to taste with salt and pepper.

To serve the soup, ladle it into warmed bowls and drizzle
with the yogurt mixture. Sprinkle with the parsley and serve
hot. *Serves 6*

Two-Onion Soup

3 tablespoons
extra-virgin olive oil

4 large yellow onions,
diced

4 leeks, including
1 inch of the tender
greens, carefully
rinsed and diced

3 oz pancetta, finely
diced (see note)

5 cloves garlic, minced

6 cups chicken stock

1¼ cups fruity red
wine, such as Chianti
or Zinfandel

2 tablespoons aged
balsamic vinegar

1 tablespoon red wine
vinegar

Salt and freshly
ground pepper

¾ cup freshly grated
Parmesan cheese

In a soup pot over medium heat, warm the olive oil. Add the onions, leeks, and pancetta and sauté, stirring occasionally, until the onions and leeks are soft, about 10 minutes. Add the garlic and sauté, stirring constantly, for 1 minute. Add the stock and simmer, uncovered, over medium-low heat, until the vegetables are very soft, about 30 minutes.

Just before serving, stir in the red wine, balsamic vinegar, and red wine vinegar. Season to taste with salt and pepper. Place over low heat until warmed through.

Ladle the soup into warmed bowls. Sprinkle the cheese equally over each serving and serve at once. *Serves 6*

NOTE: *Pancetta is a type of unsmoked bacon from Italy made by rubbing a slab of pork with a mixture of spices that include cinnamon, cloves, or juniper berries, then rolling the slab into a tight cylinder and curing it for at least 2 months.*

White Bean Soup with Smoked Ham

¾ cup dried small white, white kidney, or cannellini beans

6 fresh parsley sprigs

2 fresh thyme sprigs

2 bay leaves

1 tablespoon olive oil

¼ lb bacon, finely diced

1 yellow onion, minced

3 cloves garlic, minced

2 smoked ham hocks, 1 lb total weight

1½ cups peeled, seeded, and chopped tomatoes (fresh or canned)

6 cups chicken stock

3 tablespoons chopped fresh mint, plus mint sprigs for garnish (optional)

Salt and freshly ground pepper

Pick over the beans and discard any impurities or damaged beans. Rinse, place in a bowl, and add water to cover. Soak for 3 hours. Drain and place in a saucepan with the parsley, thyme, bay leaves, and water to cover by 2 inches. Bring to a boil over medium-high heat. Reduce the heat to low and simmer, uncovered, until nearly tender, 40–50 minutes. Drain well; discard the parsley, thyme, and bay leaves.

Meanwhile, in a soup pot over medium heat, warm the olive oil. Add the bacon and onion and sauté, stirring them occasionally, until the onion is soft, about 10 minutes. Add the garlic and continue to cook for 1 minute. Add the ham hocks, tomatoes, and chicken stock and bring to a boil. Reduce the heat to low and cook, uncovered, until the ham just begins to fall from the bone, about 1 hour. Add the beans and continue to simmer until the ham easily falls from the bones and the beans are tender, about 1 hour longer.

Remove the ham hocks from the soup and set aside until cool. Discard the skin and bones and cut the meat into ½-inch pieces. Add the ham and chopped mint to the soup, stir well, and season to taste with salt and pepper.

Ladle the soup into warmed bowls, garnish with mint sprigs if desired, and serve at once. *Serves 6*

Beet Salad with Stilton and Walnuts

1/3 cup walnut halves

2 lb red or
yellow beets

2 tablespoons olive oil

Salt and freshly
ground pepper

3 1/2 tablespoons
extra-virgin olive oil

2 1/2 tablespoons red
wine vinegar

1 1/2 cups loosely
packed watercress,
tough stems removed

3 oz Stilton cheese,
crumbled

Preheat an oven to 375°F. Spread the walnut halves on a baking sheet and toast until lightly browned and fragrant, 5–7 minutes. Remove from the oven and let cool. Leave the oven set at 375°F.

Rinse each beet with cold water and trim away all but 1/2 inch of the stem. Put the beets in a shallow baking dish and drizzle with the olive oil. Roll the beets to coat them with the oil and season with salt and pepper. Cover with aluminum foil.

Bake until the beets are tender when pierced with a knife, 50–60 minutes. Remove from the oven and set aside until cool enough to handle. Slip off the skins and cut each beet into thin wedges. Place in a bowl.

Meanwhile, in a small bowl, whisk together the extra-virgin olive oil, vinegar, and salt and pepper to taste to form a vinaigrette. Drizzle three-fourths of the vinaigrette over the beets, toss well, and let cool completely.

Place the watercress in a serving bowl, drizzle with the remaining vinaigrette, and toss to coat. Add the beets and toss again to coat. Season to taste with salt and pepper. Distribute the crumbled Stilton and the walnuts evenly over the top and serve. *Serves 6*

Winter White Salad
with Apples and Parmesan

1/2 cup walnut halves

1 1/2 tablespoons white wine vinegar

1/4 cup extra-virgin olive oil

Salt and freshly ground pepper

1 small head escarole, tough stems removed, and leaves torn into 1 1/2-inch pieces

2 heads Belgian endive, trimmed and cut lengthwise into thin strips

2 celery stalks, cut on the sharp diagonal into thin slices

1 Granny Smith, pippin, or other tart green apple, halved, cored and thinly sliced lengthwise

Shaved Parmesan cheese

Preheat an oven to 375°F. Spread the walnuts on a rimmed baking sheet and toast until lightly browned and fragrant, 5–7 minutes. Remove from the oven and let cool.

In a small bowl, whisk together the vinegar, olive oil, and salt and pepper to taste to form a vinaigrette.

In a large salad bowl, toss together the escarole, endive, and celery. Add the apple and toasted walnuts, drizzle with the vinaigrette, and toss well. Garnish with shaved Parmesan and serve at once. *Serves 6*

Citrus Salad with Mint and Red Onions

3 large navel oranges

2 blood oranges

1 Ruby grapefruit or other pink grapefruit

1/4 small red onion, very thinly sliced

3 tablespoons fresh orange juice

1 tablespoon red wine vinegar

3 tablespoons extra-virgin olive oil

Salt and freshly ground pepper

2 tablespoons coarsely chopped fresh mint

6 kumquats, thinly sliced

Pomegranate seeds for garnish (optional)

Holding 1 orange over a small bowl, finely grate enough zest to measure 1 teaspoon.

Using a sharp knife, cut a thick slice off the tops and bottoms of the navel oranges, blood oranges, and grapefruit to reveal the flesh. Working with 1 fruit at a time, place it upright on a cutting surface and cut off the peel and white membrane in wide strips. Cut the oranges and grapefruit crosswise into slices 1/4 inch thick. Cut the grapefruit slices into quarters. Using the tip of the knife, remove any seeds and discard.

Arrange the orange and grapefruit slices on a serving platter, overlapping the various colors. Separate the onion slices and scatter over the top.

Add the orange juice, vinegar, and olive oil to the bowl containing the orange zest. Season to taste with salt and pepper and whisk to form a vinaigrette. Drizzle the vinaigrette evenly over the citrus and onion. Sprinkle with the mint, kumquat slices, and pomegranate seeds (if using). Serve at once. *Serves 6*

Roast Turkey with Dried Apple and Corn Bread Stuffing

1 turkey, 10–12 lb, giblets reserved for gravy

Salt and freshly ground pepper

3/4 cup unsalted butter

2 large yellow onions, finely diced

4 celery stalks, finely diced

1 cup dried apples, coarsely chopped

1/4 cup chopped fresh flat-leaf parsley

1 tablespoon each chopped fresh thyme and sage

5–6 cups stale corn bread cubes

1 1/2 cups chicken stock

Giblet Gravy, page 60

Rinse the turkey and pat dry. Rub the turkey inside and out with 2 teaspoons salt. Preheat an oven to 400°F.

In a large frying pan over medium heat, melt 1/2 cup of the butter. Add the onions and celery and sauté until soft, about 10 minutes. Transfer to a bowl and add the apples, parsley, thyme, sage, corn bread, and stock. Stir well. Season to taste with salt and pepper.

Stuff the turkey loosely with the stuffing, then truss. Place, breast side up, on an oiled rack in a roasting pan. Melt the remaining 1/4 cup butter and brush 1 tablespoon on the turkey. Roast for 45 minutes. Soak a double layer of cheesecloth large enough to cover the turkey in the remaining butter.

Reduce the heat to 325°F. Drape the cheesecloth over the turkey and roast, basting every 30 minutes, until the juices run clear when the thickest part of the thigh is pricked or an instant-read thermometer inserted into the thigh registers 180°F, 1 1/2–2 hours longer. Remove the turkey from the oven. Let stand for 20 minutes, then transfer to a platter. Reserve 2 tablespoons fat and drippings in the pan. Make the gravy.

Carve the turkey, spoon the stuffing into a serving dish, and pass the gravy. *Serves 8*

Turkey Sandwich with Tapenade and Fontina Cheese

FOR THE TAPENADE

1 clove garlic, minced

1/2 cup pitted Niçoise olives

1 tablespoon drained capers, chopped

2 anchovy fillets, soaked in water for 5 minutes, drained, and patted dry

1 tablespoon fresh lemon juice

1 tablespoon extra-virgin olive oil

Freshly ground pepper

6 slices country-style bread

1 tablespoon extra-virgin olive oil

1 clove garlic

1 1/2 lb roasted turkey, thickly sliced

6 oz Fontina cheese, shredded

To make the tapenade, place the garlic and three-fourths of the olives in a food processor fitted with the metal blade. Process until the mixture forms a chunky paste. Add the capers and anchovies and pulse 4 or 5 times to mix. Add the remaining olives and pulse 4 or 5 times until a chunky paste again forms. Transfer to a bowl. Stir in the lemon juice and the olive oil and season to taste with pepper. You should have about 2/3 cup.

Preheat a broiler. Lightly brush the bread slices on both sides with the olive oil. Arrange in a single layer on a baking sheet. Place under the broiler 4–6 inches from the heat source and broil, turning once, until lightly golden on both sides, 30–60 seconds on each side. Lightly rub both sides of each piece of toast with the garlic clove. Divide the tapenade evenly among the bread slices and spread to cover one side of each slice completely. Distribute the turkey evenly among the bread slices. Top with the shredded cheese, again dividing evenly.

Return the pan to the broiler and broil until the cheese melts, 30–60 seconds. Serve at once. *Serves 6*

Herb-Roasted Chicken

1 roasting chicken, 3½–4 lb, giblets removed

Salt and freshly ground pepper

1 tablespoon chopped fresh sage

1 teaspoon chopped fresh thyme

½ teaspoon chopped fresh oregano

½ teaspoon chopped fresh rosemary

4 thin lemon slices, seeds removed

2 tablespoons unsalted butter, melted

Preheat an oven to 375°F. Rinse the chicken under cold water, drain, and pat dry with paper towels. Season lightly inside and outside with salt and pepper.

In a small bowl, mix together the sage, thyme, oregano, rosemary, ¼ teaspoon salt, and ⅛ teaspoon pepper. Using your fingers, loosen the skin of the chicken that covers the breast by sliding your fingers between the skin and the flesh, taking care not to tear the skin. Slip half of the herbs inside the pocket defined by each breast half and thigh. Tuck the lemon slices inside the pockets between the skin and flesh. Truss the chicken by tying the legs together with kitchen string. Brush the chicken with the melted butter.

Place the chicken on its side on an oiled roasting rack in a roasting pan. Roast for 20 minutes. Turn the chicken and roast for another 20 minutes. Turn the chicken so that it sits breast side up, and continue to roast until an instant-read thermometer inserted into the thickest part of the breast away from the bone registers 160°F and into the thigh registers 170°F, or until the juices run clear when the thigh is pierced with a knife, 15–20 minutes longer.

Remove from the oven. Cover loosely with aluminum foil and let stand for 10 minutes before carving. *Serves 4*

Pappardelle with Wine-Stewed Duck

1 tablespoon olive oil

1 duck, about 5 lb, cut into 8 pieces, skin and excess fat removed

1 large yellow onion, diced

1 large celery stalk, diced

1 large carrot, peeled and diced

3 oz pancetta, finely diced (see note, page 14)

3 cups peeled, seeded, and chopped tomatoes (fresh or canned)

2 1/2 cups dry red wine

1 tablespoon chopped fresh rosemary

Salt and freshly ground pepper

3/4 lb dried or fresh pappardelle noodles

1/2 cup freshly grated Parmesan cheese

In a large, heavy pot over medium-high heat, warm the olive oil. Add the duck and cook until it begins to turn light brown, about 10 minutes. Add the onion, celery, carrot, and pancetta and continue to cook until the onion is soft, about 10 minutes longer. Add the tomatoes, 1 1/2 cups of the red wine, and the rosemary and bring to a boil. Reduce the heat to low, cover, and simmer for 1 hour. Add the remaining 1 cup red wine, stir, and continue to simmer, uncovered, until the meat begins to fall off the bones and the sauce has thickened slightly, about 1 1/4 hours longer.

Using tongs, transfer the duck pieces to a bowl and let stand until cool enough to handle. Remove the meat from the bones and tear into bite-sized pieces; discard the bones. Return the meat to the sauce and bring to a boil. Simmer until the sauce thickens a bit more, 5–10 minutes. Season to taste with salt and pepper.

Meanwhile, bring a pot three-fourths full of salted water to a rolling boil. Add the pasta, stir well, and cook until al dente (firm but tender to the bite), 5–8 minutes. Drain and transfer to a bowl. Pour the sauce over the pasta and toss. Pass the Parmesan cheese at the table. *Serves 6*

Braised Lamb Shanks with White Beans

1½ cups dried white beans

2 tablespoons extra-virgin olive oil

6 lamb shanks, ½–¾ lb each

1 yellow onion, diced

1 celery stalk, diced

2 large carrots, peeled and finely diced

6 cloves garlic, minced

1½ cups dry red wine

1½ cups chicken stock

1½ cups peeled, seeded, and chopped tomatoes (fresh or canned)

3 tablespoons tomato paste

1 teaspoon chopped fresh thyme

1 bay leaf

Salt and freshly ground pepper

Grated lemon zest

Chopped fresh flat-leaf parsley

Pick over the beans, removing any impurities or damaged beans. Rinse the beans, place in a bowl, and add water to cover generously. Soak for about 3 hours. Drain and place in a saucepan with water to cover by about 2 inches. Place over medium-high heat and bring to a boil. Reduce the heat to low and simmer, uncovered, until nearly tender, 45–60 minutes. Drain well.

Meanwhile, in a deep, heavy pot over medium heat, warm the olive oil. Add the lamb shanks and brown on all sides, 10–12 minutes. Transfer the shanks to a plate. Add the onion, celery, and carrots to the pot and sauté over medium heat, stirring occasionally, until the onion is soft, about 10 minutes. Add the garlic and cook, stirring, for 1 minute. Add the wine, stock, tomatoes, tomato paste, thyme, bay leaf, and lamb shanks. Bring to a boil over high heat. Reduce the heat to low, cover, and simmer until the shanks can be easily pierced with a skewer, 1½–2 hours.

Add the beans, stir well, cover, and simmer gently until the lamb begins to fall from the bone and the beans are tender, about 30 minutes longer. Season to taste with salt and pepper. Remove the bay leaf and discard.

Garnish the lamb with lemon zest and parsley. Serve at once. *Serves 6*

Lobster with Tangerine-Chive Butter

FOR THE TANGERINE-
CHIVE BUTTER

3/4 cup unsalted butter

1/2 teaspoon finely
grated tangerine zest

3 tablespoons fresh
tangerine juice

1 tablespoon Dijon
mustard

1/4 cup finely snipped
fresh chives

Salt and freshly
ground pepper

FOR THE LOBSTERS

4 qt water

1 tablespoon salt

6 live lobsters,
1 1/4–1 1/2 lb each

To make the tangerine-chive butter, in a small saucepan, combine the butter, tangerine zest, tangerine juice, mustard, and chives. Season to taste with salt and pepper. Place over medium heat and, as soon as the butter melts, remove from the heat. Let stand at room temperature for 1 hour.

To prepare the lobsters, 10–15 minutes before serving, bring the water to a boil in a large stockpot. Once it boils, add the salt and the lobsters, immersing them completely. Boil until dark red and fully cooked, about 10 minutes. Using tongs, transfer to a plate and let cool slightly.

Reheat the butter until warm and divide among 6 small sauce bowls. Serve 1 lobster per person accompanied by a small bowl of the warm butter.

To make eating the lobsters easier, crack the claws and cut down the underside of the tail with heavy-duty kitchen scissors, then serve the lobster with small forks or lobster picks for extracting the meat. *Serves 6*

Crispy Salmon with Spiced Lentils

1½ cups lentils

8 whole cloves

1 small yellow onion

2 bay leaves

2 tablespoons olive oil

1 small red onion, minced

4 cloves garlic, minced

3 tomatoes, peeled, seeded, and chopped

1½ cups clam juice

1½ teaspoons each ground cumin and ground ginger

¾ teaspoon each ground turmeric and sweet paprika

¼ teaspoon ground cayenne pepper

⅓ cup each chopped fresh flat-leaf parsley and fresh cilantro

Fresh lemon juice

Salt and black pepper

6 salmon fillets, each 5–6 oz and ¾–1 inch thick, skinned

Pick over the lentils and remove any impurities or damaged lentils. Rinse well and place in a large saucepan. Add water to cover by 2 inches. Stick the cloves into the yellow onion and add to the saucepan along with the bay leaves. Bring to a boil over high heat, reduce the heat to medium-low, and simmer, uncovered, until the lentils are tender, 15–20 minutes. Drain and discard the onion and bay leaves. Set the lentils aside.

In a large frying pan over medium heat, warm about 1 tablespoon of the oil. Add the red onion and sauté, stirring occasionally, until soft, about 10 minutes. Add the garlic, tomatoes, clam juice, cumin, ginger, turmeric, paprika, and cayenne and cook uncovered, stirring occasionally, until the tomatoes are soft, about 3 minutes. Add the parsley, cilantro, and lentils and cook, stirring occasionally, until the lentils are hot, about 2 minutes. Season to taste with lemon juice, salt and black pepper. Keep warm.

Preheat a ridged cast-iron grill pan over high heat until very hot, about 15 minutes. With a pastry brush, brush the salmon with the remaining oil and place on the pan. Cook until golden and crisp on one side, 4–5 minutes. Turn over the salmon, sprinkle with salt and black pepper, and continue to cook until opaque throughout, 3–4 minutes longer. *Serves 6*

Pan-Roasted Winter Vegetables

½ lb rutabagas, peeled and cut into pieces

½ lb carrots, peeled and cut into pieces

½ lb parsnips, peeled and cut into pieces

½ lb Brussels sprouts, trimmed

½ lb sweet potatoes, peeled and cut into pieces

1 tablespoon unsalted butter

1 tablespoon extra-virgin olive oil

2 teaspoons chopped fresh thyme

2 teaspoons chopped fresh sage

⅛ teaspoon freshly grated nutmeg

Salt and freshly ground pepper

½ cup Marsala wine

Preheat an oven to 450°F.

Bring a large pot three-fourths full of salted water to a boil. Add the rutabagas, carrots, and parsnips and simmer until the vegetables give slightly when pierced with a fork, about 4 minutes. Drain well.

Place the rutabagas, carrots, parsnips, Brussels sprouts, and sweet potatoes in a large roasting pan. In a small saucepan over low heat, melt the butter. Add the olive oil, thyme, sage, and nutmeg and stir to mix well. Drizzle the butter mixture over the vegetables and toss to coat evenly. Season to taste with salt and pepper. Pour the Marsala into the bottom of the roasting pan. Cover tightly with aluminum foil.

Roast for 40 minutes. Remove the aluminum foil, toss the vegetables, and continue to roast, uncovered, until the Marsala evaporates and the vegetables can be easily pierced with a knife, 20–30 minutes.

Place the roasted vegetables on a warmed platter and serve at once. *Serves 6*

Broccoli Rabe with Pancetta and Olives

4 tablespoons olive oil

½ cup coarsely ground dried bread crumbs

Salt and freshly ground pepper

¼ lb pancetta, finely diced (see note, page 14)

3 bunches young, tender broccoli rabe, tough stems removed

3 tablespoons fresh lemon juice

3 cloves garlic, minced

½ cup Kalamata olives, pitted and chopped

In a large frying pan over medium heat, warm 2 tablespoons of the olive oil. Add the bread crumbs and toss them constantly until lightly golden, 1–3 minutes. Season to taste with salt and pepper. Transfer to a small bowl and set aside.

Pour the remaining 2 tablespoons olive oil into the frying pan and place over medium heat. Add the pancetta to the pan and cook, stirring often, until lightly golden and almost crisp, 3–4 minutes. Add the broccoli rabe and cook, stirring often, until it wilts completely but is still bright green in color, 6–8 minutes.

Raise the heat to high and add the lemon juice, garlic, and olives. Continue to cook, stirring, for 1 minute. Season to taste with salt and pepper.

Transfer to a warmed platter and sprinkle with the reserved bread crumbs. Serve at once. *Serves 6*

Braised Fennel with Olive Oil and Garlic

4 fennel bulbs, about
2 lb total weight

3 tablespoons
extra-virgin olive oil

3 cloves garlic,
chopped

1 teaspoon ground
fennel seeds

Salt and freshly
ground pepper

2 cups water

1 lemon zest strip,
about 2 inches long

2 tablespoons fresh
lemon juice

Lemon wedges

Cut off the stalks and feathery fronds from the fennel bulbs. Chop enough of the feathery fronds to measure 1 tablespoon and reserve the rest for garnish. Set aside. Remove any damaged outer leaves from the bulbs and discard. Cut each bulb into quarters lengthwise and trim away the tough core portions from the bulb.

In a large saucepan over medium heat, warm the olive oil. Add the garlic and cook, stirring, for 1 minute; do not brown. Add the fennel quarters and the fennel seeds. Season with salt and pepper. Cook uncovered, stirring occasionally, until the fennel begins to soften, about 5 minutes.

Reduce the heat to medium-low, add the water and lemon zest, cover the pan, and cook until the fennel is tender, 20–25 minutes.

Using a slotted spoon, transfer the fennel to a serving platter and keep warm. Raise the heat to high and cook until only ¾ cup liquid remains, about 5 minutes. Discard the lemon zest. Add the lemon juice, then taste and adjust the seasoning with salt and pepper.

Drizzle the sauce over the fennel and garnish with lemon wedges. Sprinkle with the chopped fennel tops and garnish with the whole fennel fronds. *Serves 6*

Golden Potato and Mushroom Gratin

½ oz dried wild mushrooms, such as porcini, chanterelles, or shiitakes

Boiling water

8 potatoes, 1¾–2 lb total weight

1½ tablespoons unsalted butter

1 lb white mushrooms, brushed clean and thinly sliced

2 teaspoons chopped fresh thyme

Salt and freshly ground pepper

3 oz good-quality blue cheese, at room temperature

2½ cups heavy cream

½ cup freshly grated Parmesan cheese

Place the dried mushrooms in a small bowl and add boiling water to cover. Let stand for 30 minutes until softened. Drain the mushrooms, chop coarsely, and set aside.

Position a rack in the upper part of an oven and preheat to 400°F. Oil a 3-qt gratin dish or other baking dish.

Thinly slice the potatoes and place in a bowl of water to cover until ready to be used. In a large frying pan over high heat, melt the butter. Add the white mushrooms, rehydrated wild mushrooms, and thyme and sauté, stirring occasionally, until the mushrooms are tender and the liquid they released has completely evaporated, 8–10 minutes. Season to taste with salt and pepper.

In a bowl, mash the blue cheese with the cream until smooth, then season to taste with salt and pepper. Place one-third of the potatoes on the bottom of the baking dish. Layer half of the mushrooms evenly over the potatoes. Add a layer of half of the remaining potatoes, and then a layer of all the remaining mushrooms. Top the mushrooms with the remaining potatoes and pour the cream mixture evenly over the top. Sprinkle evenly with the Parmesan cheese.

Bake until the potatoes are tender and the cream is almost fully absorbed, 40–50 minutes. Serve hot, spooning the gratin directly from the dish. *Serves 6–8*

Wild Rice Pilaf with Dried Fruits and Pecans

1/2 cup pecans

1 1/2 cups wild rice

3 tablespoons unsalted butter

1 small yellow onion, minced

2 1/4 cups water

2 1/4 cups chicken stock

3/4 teaspoon salt

1/4 teaspoon each ground cinnamon and ground allspice

1/8 teaspoon freshly grated nutmeg

Freshly ground pepper

1/2 cup dried apricot halves, coarsely chopped

1/4 cup golden raisins

1/4 cup dried cranberries

1/4 cup dried pitted cherries

Preheat an oven to 375°F. Spread the pecans on a rimmed baking sheet and toast until lightly browned and fragrant, about 5–7 minutes. Remove from the oven, let cool, and chop coarsely. Set aside.

Meanwhile, place the wild rice in a bowl and add water to cover. Stir the wild rice to rinse it, then drain it well and set aside. In a saucepan over medium heat, melt the butter. Add the onion to the pan and sauté, stirring occasionally, until soft, about 10 minutes. Add the wild rice, water, stock, salt, cinnamon, allspice, nutmeg, and 1/8 teaspoon pepper. Bring to a boil, reduce the heat to low, cover, and simmer gently, without stirring, until the wild rice is almost tender and most of the liquid has been absorbed, 40–45 minutes.

Add the apricots, raisins, cranberries, and cherries. Stir to combine, re-cover, and continue to cook until the wild rice is tender and all the liquid has been absorbed, 5–10 minutes longer. If the wild rice is still not tender at this point and liquid remains, re-cover and cook for a few minutes longer.

Add the pecans and toss to mix well. Season with pepper. Transfer to a bowl and serve at once. *Serves 6*

Winter Herb and Lemon Spaetzle

Unsalted butter for
the baking dish, plus
1 tablespoon unsalted
butter, melted

2 cups all-purpose
flour

3 tablespoons chopped
fresh chives

2 tablespoons chopped
fresh sage

2 tablespoons chopped
fresh flat-leaf parsley

1 tablespoon chopped
fresh thyme

2 teaspoons chopped
fresh winter savory
(optional)

1 teaspoon finely
grated lemon zest

5 eggs

2/3 cup milk

3/4 teaspoon salt

1/8 teaspoon freshly
ground pepper

Butter a large ceramic baking dish and set aside.

Place the flour, all the herbs, and the lemon zest in a bowl. In another bowl, whisk the eggs until well blended. Gradually whisk the eggs into the flour mixture. Stir in the milk, salt, and pepper. Let stand for 30 minutes.

Preheat an oven to 275°F.

Bring a large pot three-fourths full of water to a boil. Working in batches, pour some of the batter into a large colander and, using the back of a large spoon, push strips of batter into the water. Alternatively, force the batter through the holes of a spaetzle maker into the water. As soon as the dumplings float to the surface, after about 1–2 minutes, they are cooked. Using a slotted spoon, transfer the dumplings to the prepared baking dish and place them in the oven to dry the excess moisture. As each batch of dumplings is cooked, add it to the baking dish, gently tossing the freshly cooked dumplings with those already in the baking dish.

To serve, drizzle with the melted butter and toss gently to coat. Serve hot. *Serves 6*

Upside-Down Pear Gingerbread

¾ cup unsalted butter, at room temperature

1 cup firmly packed brown sugar

3 Bosc pears, peeled, cored, and thinly sliced

1 egg

¼ cup dark molasses

1½ cups all-purpose flour

2 teaspoons ground ginger

1½ teaspoons ground cinnamon

½ teaspoon baking soda

¼ teaspoon freshly grated nutmeg

¼ teaspoon ground cloves

Pinch of salt

⅓ cup boiling water

Place a 9-inch square cake pan over medium heat, add ¼ cup of the butter, and allow to melt. Add ½ cup of the brown sugar and stir just until the sugar melts. Add the pear slices and cook, stirring occasionally, until the pears just begin to soften, about 5 minutes. Arrange the pears in an even layer over the bottom of the pan and remove from the heat.

Preheat an oven to 350°F. In a bowl, using an electric mixer set on high speed, beat together the remaining ½ cup butter and ½ cup brown sugar until light and fluffy, about 3 minutes. Add the egg and molasses and beat until well mixed, about 1 minute. Into another bowl, sift together the flour, ginger, cinnamon, baking soda, nutmeg, cloves, and salt. Dividing the flour mixture into 2 batches, and using a rubber spatula, fold the flour mixture into the butter-sugar mixture alternately with the water, beginning and ending with the flour. Do not overmix.

Spoon the batter over the pears. Bake until springy to the touch, 30–40 minutes. Remove from the oven and let cool on a rack for about 5 minutes. Carefully invert the cake onto a serving plate. Cut into squares and serve warm or at room temperature. *Serves 9*

Cinnamon-Poached Quinces
with Nutmeg Cream

8 cups water

2 cups granulated sugar

5 cinnamon sticks

5 quinces, about 10 oz each, peeled, halved, cored, and cut into eighths

1 cup heavy cream

1 tablespoon confectioners' sugar

1/2 teaspoon freshly grated nutmeg

In a large saucepan over high heat, combine the water, granulated sugar, and cinnamon sticks. Bring to a boil, stirring occasionally, and add the quinces to the pan. Reduce the heat to low and simmer, uncovered, until the quinces are tender and have turned a deep rose color, 2–2 1/2 hours. Add water during cooking if necessary to keep the fruit covered with liquid. Do not stir the quinces while they are simmering; instead, move them about gently if necessary for even cooking.

Before serving, in a large bowl, using a whisk or an electric mixer, beat the cream until soft peaks form. Stir in the confectioners' sugar and the nutmeg until blended. Cover and refrigerate to chill until serving.

To serve, using a slotted spoon, transfer the warm quinces to a bowl. Serve the cream on the side. *Serves 6*

Baked Apples with Calvados Custard Sauce

6 apples, such as Golden Delicious, Cortland, Rome Beauty, or McIntosh

1/2 cup firmly packed light brown sugar

4 tablespoons unsalted butter, at room temperature

1/2 cup water

1/2 teaspoon ground cinnamon

1/2 teaspoon grated lemon zest

1/2 cup walnuts

1/3 cup dried apples, chopped

Calvados Custard Sauce, page 61

Preheat an oven to 375°F. Peel the top one-fourth of each apple, leaving the stem intact. Cut a slice 1/2 inch thick off the stem ends and set aside. Core the apples, cutting to within 1/2 inch of the base but leaving the base intact.

In a small pan over medium-high heat, combine 1/4 cup of the brown sugar, 2 tablespoons of the butter, the water, 1/4 teaspoon of the cinnamon, and the lemon zest. Bring to a boil. Remove from the heat and set aside.

Spread the walnuts on a baking sheet and toast until lightly golden and fragrant, 5–7 minutes. Let cool, chop coarsely, and place in a bowl. Add the dried apples and the remaining 1/4 cup brown sugar, remaining 1/4 teaspoon cinnamon, and remaining 2 tablespoons butter. Stir to mix well. Fill the apples with the mixture. Replace the stem ends.

Arrange the apples in a 2-qt baking dish and pour the brown sugar syrup over them. Cover and bake until nearly tender, about 30 minutes. Uncover, baste with the pan juices, and bake until easily pierced, about 15 minutes longer.

Remove from the oven, drizzle with the pan juices, and slip under a preheated broiler for about 1 minute. Spoon the sauce onto plates and place an apple in the center. *Serves 6*

Caramel Pots de Crème

1 cup sugar

1/3 cup plus 1/4 cup water

1 1/2 cups heavy cream

1 1/2 cups milk

8 egg yolks

Boiling water, as needed

Place the sugar and the 1/3 cup water in a heavy saucepan over medium-high heat. Cover and bring to a boil. Uncover the pan and cook until the sugar turns golden amber in color, 8–12 minutes. Be careful, as the caramel is very hot.

Combine the cream and milk in a large saucepan over medium-high heat and warm until small bubbles appear along the edges of the pan. Remove from the heat.

Preheat an oven to 325°F. Add the remaining 1/4 cup water to the caramel and whisk vigorously until the bubbles subside. Pour the caramel into the hot cream mixture and whisk together until mixed. Let cool for about 10 minutes.

In a bowl, whisk together the egg yolks. Slowly add the caramel mixture, stirring constantly until mixed. Strain through a fine-mesh sieve into a measuring pitcher.

Pour the custard into six 2/3-cup ramekins. Place the ramekins in a baking pan. Pour boiling water into the pan to reach about 1 inch up the sides of the ramekins. Bake until the edges of the custards are set, 40–50 minutes. Remove the baking pan from the oven and transfer to a rack to cool for about 10 minutes.

Remove the custards from the water bath and let cool. Refrigerate for several hours or overnight until well chilled. Serve chilled or at room temperature. *Serves 6*

Spiced Pumpkin Pie

1 small pumpkin,
2½ lb

Basic Pie Pastry,
page 61

¼ cup maple syrup

¼ cup firmly packed
light brown sugar

1½ teaspoons ground
cinnamon

1 teaspoon ground
ginger

½ teaspoon ground
nutmeg

¼ teaspoon ground
cloves

3 eggs, beaten

¾ cup half-and-half

Sweetened whipped
cream

Preheat an oven to 350°F. Lightly oil a baking sheet. Cut the pumpkin in half through the stem end and place, cut side down, on the baking sheet. Bake until easily pierced with a knife, about 1 hour. Let cool. Scoop out the seeds and fibers and discard. Purée the flesh in a food processor fitted with the metal blade until smooth. Measure out 1½ cups; set aside. Raise the oven temperature to 375°F.

Make the pastry. On a well-floured work surface, roll out the pastry into a 12-inch round. Transfer to a 9-inch pie pan and gently press into the bottom and sides of the pan. Trim the edges, leaving a 1½-inch overhang, then fold under the overhang and crimp to form an attractive rim. Prick the bottom and sides of the pastry with a fork. Freeze for 10 minutes.

Line the pastry with aluminum foil and fill with pie weights. Bake for 15 minutes. Remove the weights and foil and continue to bake until lightly golden, 10–15 minutes. Transfer to a rack and let cool. Leave the oven set at 375°F.

In a bowl, whisk together the pumpkin purée, maple syrup, brown sugar, cinnamon, ginger, nutmeg, cloves, eggs, and half-and-half until well mixed. Pour into the baked pie shell. Bake until a skewer inserted into the center comes out clean, 45–55 minutes. Let cool for at least 30 minutes. Serve the pie with the whipped cream on the side. *Serves 6–8*

Seasonal Basics

SOUR CREAM PASTRY

1¼ cups all-purpose flour, chilled

¼ teaspoon salt

½ cup frozen unsalted butter, cut into pieces

¼ cup sour cream

2 teaspoons fresh lemon juice

¼ cup ice water

Put the flour and salt in a bowl. Add the butter and, using a pastry blender, cut it in until the mixture resembles coarse meal. In another bowl, whisk together the sour cream, lemon juice, and water and add half of this mixture to the flour mixture. With your fingertips, mix in the liquid until large lumps form. Remove the lumps and repeat the process with the remaining liquid and flour-butter mixture. Pat all the lumps into a ball; do not overwork the dough. Wrap in plastic and refrigerate for 1 hour. *Makes one 10-inch pie shell*

GIBLET GRAVY

Giblets from one 10–12 lb turkey

5 cups chicken stock

1 yellow onion, diced

1 carrot, peeled and diced

6 fresh parsley sprigs, ¼ teaspoon dried thyme, and 1 bay leaf

1 tablespoon all-purpose flour

1 teaspoon cornstarch

Roasting pan from the turkey with 2 tablespoons fat and drippings

Place the giblets in a saucepan and add the stock, onion, carrot, and herbs. Bring to a boil, reduce the heat to low, and simmer until the liquid is reduced by two-thirds, about 1½ hours. Strain through a sieve.

Place the turkey roasting pan with the drippings over high heat. Whisk together the flour, cornstarch, and ½ cup of the reduced stock, then whisk into the pan. Add the remaining stock and stir until thickened, about 2 minutes. Simmer for 1 minute and strain through a fine-mesh sieve into a sauceboat; keep warm. *Makes 1½ cups*

CALVADOS CUSTARD SAUCE

4 egg yolks

2 cups milk

1/4 cup sugar

1/4 teaspoon vanilla extract

2 tablespoons Calvados or
other dry apple brandy

In a bowl, whisk the egg yolks until
blended. In a saucepan over medium-
high heat, combine the milk and sugar
and heat, stirring until the sugar
dissolves. When small bubbles appear
along the edges of the pan, slowly whisk
the milk mixture into the egg yolks.
Pour the mixture back into the pan and
return it to medium heat. Cook, stirring
the mixture constantly, just until it
thickens and coats the back of a spoon,
3–4 minutes. Immediately remove from
the heat and strain through a fine-mesh
sieve into a bowl. Stir in the vanilla and
brandy. *Makes 6 servings*

BASIC PIE PASTRY

1 1/2 cups all-purpose flour

1 tablespoon sugar

1/2 teaspoon salt

1/2 cup unsalted butter, chilled,
cut into pieces

3 tablespoons vegetable shortening,
chilled, cut into pieces

3 tablespoons ice water

In a bowl, mix together the flour,
sugar, and salt. Add the butter and
shortening and, using your fingertips,
rub them into the flour mixture until
small, flat pieces form. Sprinkle on the
water and gently mix with a fork.
Gather the dough into a rough ball; do
not overwork. Wrap in plastic and
refrigerate for 2 hours. *Makes one
9-inch pie shell*

Index

First published in the USA in 1997
by Time-Life Custom Publishing.

Originally published in 2 volumes titled
Autumn and *Winter* (both copyright © 1997
Weldon Owen Inc.).

In collaboration with Williams-Sonoma Inc.
3250 Van Ness Avenue, San Francisco, CA 94109

WILLIAMS-SONOMA
Founder & Vice-Chairman: Chuck Williams
Book Buyer: Cecilia Prentice
Assistant Book Buyer: India Leval

WELDON OWEN INC.
Chief Executive Officer: John Owen
President: Terry Newell
Chief Operating Officer: Larry Partington
Creative Director: Gaye Allen
Publisher: Hannah Rahill
Editor: Jennifer Newens
Assistant Editor: Donita Boles
Design: Charlene Charles
Production Director: Chris Hemesath
Proofreader: Desne Ahlers
Indexer: Ken DellaPenta
Food and Prop Stylist: Pouké

Williams-Sonoma Seasonal Favorites
Conceived and produced by
Weldon Owen Inc.
814 Montgomery Street
San Francisco, CA 94133

A Weldon Owen Production
Copyright © 2002 Weldon Owen Inc.
and Williams-Sonoma Inc.

First printed in 2002
10 9 8 7 6 5 4 3 2 1

Color separations by Colourscan Overseas
Company (Pte.) Ltd.
Printed and bound in Singapore by Tien Wah
Press (Pte.) Ltd